experimental musical instruments

ORBITONES SPOON HARPS & BELLOWPHONES

Written and Produced by

Bart Hopkin

ellipsis arts...

ORBITONES, Spoon Harps & Bellowphones

Written and Produced by
BART HOPKIN

Project Director
RUSSELL CHARNO D.C.

Executive Producer
JEFFREY CHARNO

Editor
WILL HERMES

Graphic Design
ONLINE COLOUR GRAPHICS NYC

For a catalog, contact:

Ellipsis Arts...
P.O. Box 305
Roslyn, NY 11576
Phone: (800) 788-6670
Fax: (516) 621-2727
Email: Elliarts@aol.com

Front Cover Photos: *(clockwise)*
The Majestic Bellowphone photo by Tim Lynch
The Stamenphone, Bellwheels
photo by Helge Pedersen
Huaca photo by Richard Sargent
Spoon Harp photo by Sven Wiederholt
Gram Pan photo by Cristiano Quintino
Kotar photo by Alain Sabatier
Great Island Mouthbow photo by Spiral Sound
Stiltophone photo by Les Phônes
Printed and bound by:
R.R.Donnelley & Sons in Mexico

Back Cover Photos:
Arthea photos by Alain Sabatier

ellipsis arts...

TABLE OF CONTENT

FOREWORD

My career as a synthesizer designer began in the first days of 1964. Before then my experience with electronic musical instruments was confined to designing and building theremins, which are instruments that you play by moving your hands in the space around them, without touching them at all.

In December of 1963 I met Herbert Deutsch at a music teachers' convention near New York City. Herb, who was interested in using electronics to explore the musical potential of new sounds, asked me if I knew anything about electronic music. I said yes, a little. He told me of his compositional interests and we talked about the possibility of working together. Herb then invited me to his next concert, which was to be in a few weeks at the studio of a colleague of his, the sculptor Jason Seley.

I saw an amazing sight when I showed up at Jason's studio on the appointed day. On the stage were several of Jason's sculptures. They were large pieces, made of automobile bumpers which were meticulously welded together to form wonderful soaring surfaces, like wing sections of some fantastic giant prehistoric steel birds. They glowed and shimmered in the subdued stage lighting, waiting silently for the audience to be seated and the musicians to step on the stage.

Well, Seley's sculptures didn't stay silent for long. One of Herb's

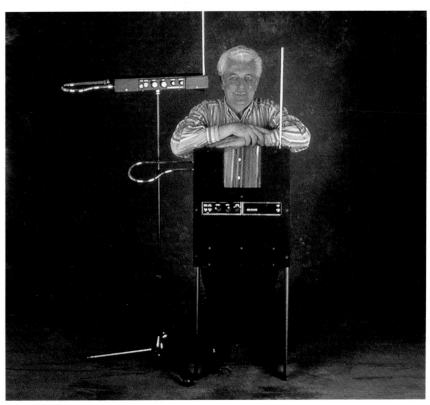

Robert Moog with the Etherwave Theramin and the Big Bria Theramin Model 91B

pieces was for percussionist and tape recorder. Percussionist Steve Elmer played the usual battery of percussion instruments. But he also played the sculptures! With sticks, mallets, and brushes, he drew a breathtaking range of sounds from the chrome bumpers which Seley had snagged on their way to Car Heaven. It was sculpture, music, and dance, all at once and all together, with Steve's motions interacting with the shapes of Seley's pieces.

I remember leaving Herb's concert with a sense of exhilaration. I was turned on to the sounds of car bumpers, and how, when formed into visually interesting shapes and played in a musical way, these common metal pieces, that would ordinarily have been chopped up and melted down , were now reborn into implements of musical expression. Besides that, I felt that I now understood and appreciated Herb's musical vision.

A few months after that concert, Herb and I got together to try out some electronic circuits that I designed for him. I showed him how to use the circuits to create new sound contours and textures, and Herb used his tape recorder to assemble the sounds into short pieces of electronic music. By the summer of 1964, Herb had several compositions on tape, and we had developed the basic ideas for what would evolve into the Moog electronic music synthesizers. By the close of 1964, I had shown my new circuits (which I called 'voltage-controlled electronic music modules' back then) to many musicians, several of whom placed orders, and I was off and running in the synthesizer business.

What was going on here? Was I merely an electronically inventive nerd, amusing myself by slapping various combinations of transistors, capacitors, and resistors together to come up with circuits that nobody had ever thought of before? And was Herb just trying to rattle listeners' cages by assembling sequences of strange, weird sounds? No, not at all! We started with Herb's musical vision, a sense that electronically-produced sounds could be musically expressive.

We then drew in my intuitive feel for the sonic capabilities of electronic circuits, which I had developed as a result of many years of designing and building theremins. On the way we found that each circuit had its own musical quality and response. You could hear it, and you could feel it, just as surely as a violinist feels the response of a fine violin, or the quality of its tone. We were making the same sort of musical discoveries that percussionist Steve Elmer was making with Jason Seley's bumper sculptures at Herb's concert. We were starting with sonic vibrations of physical structures, then going in two directions from there. Herb was exploring new musical relationships, while

I was exploring new circuits. It was an interactive exploration for us — Herb fed ideas for new circuits to me, and every new circuit that I designed gave Herb some musical inspiration.

I didn't realize it at the time, but what Herb and I were doing was right in sync with the musical mainstream. Musically speaking, the twentieth century has been a time of fascination with new sounds. Musicians have developed new techniques for playing traditional instruments, electronic music synthesizers have added virtually unlimited new timbral resources, and sample-players have put the sounds of the world at the musician's fingertips. The development of new musical sounds — 'Sound Design' — is now a specialty of its own.

Herb and I were Sound Designers of a sort, even before the term was invented. And lots of other musicians and technicians have been doing the same thing. In the 'serious music' arena of the concert hall and the academic laboratory, the design and development of new ways of making musical sounds have dominated the past fifty years or so, while in pop and commercial music, the novelty and excitement of the musical sounds themselves have assumed paramount importance.

Today we tend to think of Sound Design, the development of new musical sounds and ways of producing them, as something one does with electronic technology. That's what it usually is, especially in the commercial music realm. But it's not always electronic. As a process, Sound Design is the building of connections between a technical resource and an artistic vision. It's fun to do with electronics, but in some ways it's even more fun to do without electronics, using mechanical devices and structures that we find or invent. Bart Hopkin has collected the stories and works of an amazing group of musician-technicians who have combined finely-tuned technical intuition with musical creativity and theatrical flair. They have developed completely new instruments, and have taught themselves to play these instruments. I think of them as 'Alternate Sound Designers', people who have followed their own unique ideas of how to make their contributions to the current musical mainstream. And what better person is there to tell these stories than Bart Hopkin, whose periodicals and books on experimental and self-made musical instruments have been an inspiration to me and many thousands of other music technology explorers. ✦

Robert Moog

of the most imaginative, inventive and ingenious people working in recent years in the field of creative musical instrument design.

This is actually one of two such collections. Its companion, *Gravikords, Whirlies and Pyrophones*, featured a cast of artisan-musicians of wildly differing persuasions — makers of winds, strings, percussion, electronic instruments and other less-categorizable types, playing music as varied as their instruments, all of it fresh in concept and fresh in sound. Here in this second set, we'll follow a similarly eclectic agenda in the continuing pursuit of instruments strange and new.

One of the special things about any new instrument is

T his book and its accompanying CD are devoted to makers of musical instruments. Gathered here, in text and photos and sound, you will find instruments and music from some

tone quality: how its sound differs from that of others that have come before. New musical approaches can take shape in new sound, and old approaches can take on new life. Many factors contribute to an instrument's characteristic sound, and it can be rewarding to learn, with practice, to hear and appreciate how these factors work together to give an intriguing sound its distinctive flavor. When it comes to this sort of close listening, our ears are smarter — more sophisticated, that is, in interpreting the information that comes to them — than we usually give them credit for.

Here's an example of ear-intelligence of a sort that might often be overlooked:

I have always been intrigued by splashes, and curious as to how they take the particular forms they do. I used to study splashes by eye, throwing stones into ponds or streams and watching closely in the crucial moments after the rock hits the surface. But things happened too fast, and some of the action was concealed by surrounding water. At some point, I had the idea of listening rather than looking. I tossed a stone, and another and another, closing my eyes and focusing entirely on the sound. I got two things out of this exercise. I did indeed develop an understanding of splash mechanics well beyond what I had arrived at by eye alone. (I'd take you through my aural interpretation of a typical splash, instant by instant and

Stomp's "Lid Combat"

sound by sound, but my space is limited here.) The other thing I got out of the splash-listening was just this: I discovered that with a little extra focus I was able to hear the sound in unexpectedly rich detail, and that the sound, heard this way, was very beautiful.

Two of the essential factors that contribute to the character of a sound are the mixtures of frequencies within the tone, and the ways in which the relative strengths of different requencies change through time. Let's look for a moment at this question of frequencies, particularly as it relates to musical instruments. Most

Ela Lamblin's Rumitone

15

sounds are made up not of a single vibrational frequency, but of many frequencies forming a complex blend. In the majority of familiar musical , the frequencies that make up the blend fall into a pattern known as the *harmonic series*.

Typically the lowest of the frequencies, known as the *fundamental*, is the one that the ear recognizes as the defining pitch, while the others form a particular pattern of overtones above it. Well made wind instruments usually meet this description; so do string instruments as long as the strings aren't misshapen. Marimbas and kalimbas do not, unless (as is done with Western orchestral marimbas) the bars or tines are specially reshaped to bring the lower overtones into agreement with tones in the series.

Arthea's Altars

In Western music, instruments with harmonic overtones have been seen as the norm and the ideal. But if you're interested in really unusual sounds, inharmonic may be the way to go. In the 1930s, the late American composer John Cage was looking in that direction, composing for distinctly non-harmonic me-tallic constructions including brake drums and tin cans, gongs and more. The most exciting of his explorations into inharmonic tone qualities came with his development around 1940 of what he called prepared piano. His idea was to modify the sound of a piano by attaching things to the strings in ways that would drastically alter their tone color. Lovely and exotic sonorities emerged from that most staid of instruments under Cage's preparations. And, of course, these timbres were brazenly out of line with the harmonic series. On the accompanying CD, you can hear these sounds in "Sonata #XIV" from Cage's *Sonatas and Interludes for Prepared Piano*. Listen to them closely: you can almost see the renegade overtone components within the peculiar tones like colors in a kaleidoscope.

Many of the other instruments to be heard in this collection are inharmonic as well — as, for instance, much of ZGA's crazy crashing noise, Ela Lamblin's glittering percussions, or Les Phônes' randomly melodic *Pongophone*. Ellen Fullman's extraordinary *Long String Instrument*, on the other hand, is purely, perfectly harmonic. You can clearly hear the different harmonic overtones rising at different times to the fore within the tone as she makes her sustained strokes on the strings. Colin Offord's *Mouthbow*, too, produces a harmonic timbre, and in its peculiar *wah-wah* sound you can hear him bringing out and emphasizing different harmonics through his vocal-cavity-resonance technique.

This business of harmonic versus inharmonic overtones is just one among many facets of an instrument's personality. And whether this short discussion will be helpful in illuminating that facet I don't know. Perhaps a better approach would be for all of us to go and listen to a few splashes. But I've raised these ssues in an effort to encourage you to listen to this CD with ears open to sound worlds that may lie half-hidden. So open, and read, and look, and listen. And to continue when you're done, perhaps you can find a nearby pond or stream ... +

THE ARTISTS

ZGA
ZGAMONIUMS

Nick Soudnick is the founder of the musical group ZGA, and the maker of the sound instruments he refers as *Zgamoniums*. The group, which has featured a changing cast over the years, started in Riga, Latvia in 1984. There, living and practicing in a crowded apartment building, the musicians found themselves unable play aloud for fear of disturbing neighbors. (Much of ZGA's music, as you'll understand when you listen to their track on the accompanying CD, is forceful and robust.) So Nick took to contact-miking his sound sources in a way that turned a small acoustic sound within the room into a big sound in the headphones and on the recording tape.

In 1991, Nick left Latvia for St. Petersburg, partly in order to take advantage of better practice spaces and recording facilities. Noise restrictions would no longer be such a problem, but the contact mics, and the particular sound qualities he had learned to coax out of them, remained an essential part of ZGA's music. That music is characterized by a big, resonant, echoey sound; rough and edgy, and still at times finely delineated and delicate. Some of it has clear tonal centers and moments of melody, while some is made entirely of sounds without pitch. The unpitched pieces have the feeling of abstract paintings — the sort where you sense in the relations of shape and color that the artist is onto something, even if you can't say what.

Nick occasionally plays clarinet or accordion in addition to the instruments that he has made, and in some pieces his dark voice breaks the surface. Toy reeds, whistles, combs and such find their way in as well. Electric guitar and bass may be present, in the hands of some very skilled players too — but played in a manner closely allied to the sound qualities of the zgamoniums.

Members of ZGA playing the Zgamoniums

So what are zgamoniums? They are mostly metal objects, made from scrap. "When I find something that could be interesting for sound," Nick says, "I take it with me. And I have many, many, many of these kinds of things in my workshop." For several of the instruments, a primary sounding element is steel springs. They may be stretched between bars in a steel frame, or across the surface of a table-like structure. Sometimes several springs of different weights and diameters are joined together, or connected with strings. Strings may also be attached separately, alongside the springs. In one instrument an old wooden zither, well-worn but seemingly whole, sits conspicuously among the other attachments. The strings and springs can be plucked, scraped, struck or bowed.

Other zgamoniums employ plates of steel or other metals. These come in all kinds of found-object shapes, and they're mounted in different ways — sometimes separately suspended, leaving them free to vibrate, sometimes held rigidly, sometimes attached fast to each other or fixed loosely so they can rattle together. One of the instruments has many smaller, thicker metal plates or disks supported on heavy springs mounted on a wooden table.

Springs and metal plates are alike in this respect: both typically have relatively little acoustic damping, and they tend to produce sustained, multifrequency resonances. When many different springs and strings and plates are joined together, as they are in the zgamoniums, they interact to produce especially complex vibrating systems. Everything is connected; all the parts share their resonances and serve as soundboards for each other. To the ear, the results are, in a sense, chaotic — no simple, harmonious pitch relationships here — but chaotic, in the ZGA players' hands, in gritty and always interesting ways.

"Most important," Nick maintains, "are the special piezo elements" — the contact mics which, he says, impart a distinctive character to the amplified sound. The ones he uses are not designed for musical purposes. They are used in Russia as a type of signaling device, sending a single electrical impulse when, for instance, a piece of glass to which they had been attached is broken. But on an instrument, Nick says, "they work like a pickup, and a very interesting pickup." Each instrument is wired with several of them, attached at selected locations on the body and sounding elements of the instrument to pick up the different resonances.

The zgamoniums often undergo changes, with Nick reconfiguring them for different pieces of music or different musical effects. He doesn't care about looks, he says. It's just the sound he's after; that and portability. But people who've seen ZGA in performance describe the visual effect as riveting. ("They looked like a scrap yard up there!" one concert-goer remarked.)

"Back to the East," the ZGA piece included on the accompanying CD, was recorded in St. Petersburg in 1995. Nick is joined by musicians Scarlett and Michael Judenich playing a variety of sound objects and instruments. The recording is dedicated to Alexander Zhylin, an essential part of ZGA for many years, who had died the previous year. ✦

Zgamoniums

23

COLIN OFFORD

GREAT ISLAND MOUTHBOW, EAGLE FEATHER FLUTE AND MORE

"I sometimes liken Australian artists to the platypus," says Colin Offord. He believes that to thrive as an artist Down Under, one must, like the egg-laying,

Colin Offord playing the Eagle Feather Flute

pouch-cheeked and duck-billed mammal, be many things at once, able to fill many different roles as opportunities arise. At the same time, like artists everywhere, one must find one's own voice and be one's own kind of animal.

It's safe to say that Colin Offord is his own kind of artist. And he does fill many roles: leader of his group The Great Island Bowing Company, soloist, educator — and, of course, instrument maker. Colin's primary instrument, made very much in the many-things-at-once spirit of the platypus, is his *Great Island Mouthbow*. The term "mouthbow," among people who study musical instruments, refers to a device typically consisting of a single string stretched on a bowed piece of wood, and played with one end up against the teeth, cheek or jaw. The player's mouth serves as an air-chamber-type resonator, and the player can, by moving the mouth to alter the size and shape of the oral cavity, selectively bring out different overtones within the string's sound. The string's fundamental pitch is always present, repetitiously sounding the same underlying tone, but a faint melody can be heard in the play of the selected overtones above. Such instruments have long been made and played in many parts of the world.

The Great Island Mouthbow operates on the same principle, but it's a mouthbow with a difference. His instrument had its beginnings in 1980 (Colin credits instrument inventor Terry Hennessy for the seed of the idea), and it has gone through several incarnations since. In its current form it has five strings mounted on a stick-like body about four feet long, made of a branch of the paperbark tree which remains in near-natural form. The instrument is held, player standing, like a guitar with a strap. The strings can be plucked or bowed or played by striking with chopsticks. Connected to the bridge at one end of the strings is a system by which the vibrations from the strings are transmitted to a pair of small diaphragms and, from there, into a tube leading up to the player's mouth. The player can bring out different overtones, mouthbow style, by changing the shape of the mouth.

Colin's mouthbow has a number of other sound-features as well: a bell and a small cymbal, a fork flattened so that its tines work like the keys of a *kalimba*, a guiro-like row of ridges carved into the wood of the body, some coil springs, two small wheels that can add spinning sounds or buzzing sounds. And there are the feathers — long, beautiful bush turkey and pheasant feathers flaring out from one end and making no sound at all.

The heart of the instrument is the string-and-mouth resonating system. The key to this system — and it is a very subtle business — is in the balance of materials at each step in the sound-transmission chain. As with any string instrument, the mouthbow radiates sound from the instrument body. This body sound must not be allowed to overwhelm the subtler overtones selectively

> **"THE MOUTHBOW — IT'S JUST SUCH AN ECLECTIC BEAST. I DELIBERATELY WANTED TO BRING TOGETHER MANY INSTRUMENTS INTO ONE."**

Colin Offord playing the Great Island Mouthbow

resonated at the mouth, and so the mouth tones must be brought to the fore as much as possible. "The reason it works," Colin says, "is because I've put a lot of time into the marriage of the different materials." When the marriage is right, "everything hums; everything is designed to sing off of everything else." You can hear the Great Island Mouthbow, with its waves of rising and falling overtones, in Colin's track "Heavenly Flower" in the accompanying CD.

The other featured instrument in that track is his *Eagle Feather Flute*. Recalling the first such flute he made, Colin says "In 1987, I was given the left wing feather of an Australian Wedge-Tailed Eagle. I kept it for many months, thinking that it was so beautiful that I didn't want to use it just as a decoration. And when I wasn't watching, as it were, the thought arrived in my mind that it should sing like a bird." The quill of the feather, with the insides cleaned out and with a series of fingerholes added, makes a narrow-bore, high-pitched flute of soaring tone, penetrating but not harsh in sound.

Colin has produced many other instruments for himself and for his performance group, the Great Island Bowing Company. His *Moonbells* are heavy aluminum and brass chimes in moon-like shapes suspended in a frame. The *Xylopt* is a growing family of natural bailer

Colin Offord in performance

shells, some small and some very large, set on pads and struck with soft mallets to create varied tones. The windpipes are a set of flute-like aluminum pipes, each capable of multiple tones from the harmonic overtone series. Some have added fingerholes; some have kazoo-like buzzing membranes; some have stopped ends and others have open ends, bringing a variety of flute sounds and playing gestures together in a single instrument set. Colin also often plays conch shell in performance.

"You find that when most Australian artists talk about their work, they end up talking about the landscape," observes Colin. Speaking of his home terrain in the Blue Mountains of New South Wales, he continues, "The landscape is characterized by this wild, un-

Naomi Vaughan with Moon Bells

controllable, ancient force of nature. It has been a profound influence, certainly, on my work." Of course, one cannot truly reproduce the vastness of the land in art. But for Colin, a keyword is "respond." "I wanted an instrument — and I wanted a music — that responded to the world I live in." +

TOM WAITS

SEWING MACHINES, SQUEAKY DOORS AND THE SPIN CYCLE

Tom Waits is not as much a builder of musical instruments as he is a finder of sounds. "I was just getting a tire put on my car," he says. "I was in the garage, and they were fixing a flat, and I was listening to the sound of the tire machine — the hydraulic machine that pushes the tire down and lets the air out — and all the tools involved. I turned my tape recorder on, and I got some amazing sounds. I mean the tire machine is just a little machine, but in the echo of the garage it sounds like something from the industrial revolution."

You can hear other discoveries in his track on the enclosed CD. The underlying rhythm in "Babbachichuija" is provided by a sewing machine. Offset against that are door squeaks, and around and between you can hear the washing machine in its spin cycle. The experimental musical instrument for which Tom Waits is best known — his voice — is in there too, riding over the rest in an incantation of unknown meaning.

Waits is interested in sound in and of itself, in all its incidental shapes and forms. He finds himself, for instance, attracted to the work of sound artists for films: "The kind of things they do are often thankless and hidden," he notes. "They'll be out laying by the side of Interstate 5 in the bushes at three in the morning to get the sound of a truck going by ... or close-up sounds of insect rituals ..."

The sounds that fill Tom's recordings, however, don't appear only as sound for sound's sake, even when their sources are hard to identify. Always

"IT'S OPENED UP THE EYES OF MY EARS."

Tom Waits

central in his work are emotion, drama and humor; all organized as music. No abstract sound collage here: these are basic song forms finding their impetus in folk-based rhythms familiar to everyone. All is steeped in humanity, colored by context and meaning. In this sense, Tom stands opposite another of the musicians included in this collection, John Cage, who sought to apprehend sound independent of human frames of reference and to unburden it of human intent.

In his earlier years, Tom's musical output came through conventional instruments. It's only in recent years that odd and improbable sound sources have appeared in his recordings. He mixes them with more familiar instruments, as well as lesser-known traditional and folk instruments. The music all takes shape, in his words, as "a journal of half-familiar maladies." A good share of the credit, he notes, goes to his wife Kathleen Brennan, with whom he collaborates on the songs, sounds and lyrics.

Tom also has picked up musical instruments from a number of experimental instrument makers to use in performances and recordings. "I love Q. Reed Ghazala and his Tesla-like devices. I own one of his *Photon Clarinets* and incorporated it into the Robert Wilson opera *Alice* that Kathleen and I did the music for." He also mentions Tom Nunn's *Bug*, an instrument arranged like a little table with lots of small, commonplace sound-making elements attached: combs, threaded rods, friction surfaces, stretched strings and the like — each one different in the sounds it makes, and each seeming to say "play me!"

For him, playing the Bug is instinctive. "You don't have to know how to pick prunes," he says. "You just say to yourself 'which one do I pick first?' I love that. And you don't need any background in music in order to play it, and I love that as well." ✦

BILL COLVIG
& LOU HARRISON

AMERICAN GAMELAN

Many American composers, particularly on the West Coast, have been captivated and deeply influenced by *gamelan* music. The word

Bill Colvig and Lou Harrison

"gamelan" refers to the orchestra of instruments used in Javanese and Balinese classical music. A typical gamelan is centered around an array of tuned gongs and chimes, augmented by bowed or plucked strings, flute and drum. The music is unlike any other. To Western ears it often has a dreamy and floating quality, though a highly formalized structure underlies it.

One of the first among American composers to take an interest in gamelan was Lou Harrison, who began to seriously study the music of Asia and the Pacific in the 1960s. Lou was already, by then, a composer of stature. A list of his professional affiliations would include the leading names in 20th century American classical music: he had studied as a young man with Henry Cowell and Arnold Schoenberg; he later edited, to much critical approval, the scores of Charles Ives; he had worked with, or maintained close correspondences with, Virgil Thomson and John Cage.

At the same time, Lou had an affinity for music that leaned away from the complexity and abstractness of mid-century modernism. Latin American and Native American musical styles held a special place in his heart, as did the simpler, more open-textured European music of the pre-Baroque. In the many varieties of Asian music he found a spaciousness that echoed his own predisposition toward open textures, a singleness of line that reflected his sense of the primacy of melody, and a blending of sounds that answered his feeling for pure sonority. And

so, at a time when the academic currents of modern classical music remained preoccupied with a highly abstract European-derived notion of compositional procedure, Lou Harrison followed both his intellect and his heart in a different direction, westward across the Pacific.

It was around this time, in 1967, that Lou began to work with Bill Colvig in

what was to become a longstanding professional association. Bill was not, at the time, a maker of musical instruments. He was working as an electrician — albeit an electrician with a strong interest and solid background in music. With Lou's musical ideas tending increasingly toward sonorities not available in the Western orchestra, Bill stepped in to fill a need, and took on the role of instrument maker.

Their first major project was the construction of what they initially referred to as "An American Gamelan:" an ensemble of mostly metallic instruments inspired by the traditional gamelan, but not intended to replicate it. This instrument set, now referred to as *Old Granddad* (because it was the first of several that Bill and Lou have conceived and constructed over the years), can be heard in the accompanying CD. The movement titled "Jhala III" from Lou's *Suite for Violin and American Gamelan* (1974) was selected for inclusion on the CD because it presents — and presents so very deliciously — this first, and in some ways most unique, of the Colvig/Harrison gamelans. In this movement, with the violin tacit, we hear Bill's instruments alone.

While later gamelans from Bill and Lou are modeled more closely on traditional Indonesian gamelan, Old Granddad takes its own direction. "Our primary consideration," Bill has said, "was to make beautiful sound; our primary purpose to build a usable musical instrument for which serious music could be composed."

Electrical metal tubing, the widely available steel conduit used for running electrical wires, was familiar to Bill from his days as an electrician, and proved an excellent material for sounding elements. The conduit instruments have sections of the tubing, tuned by cutting to length, arranged xylophone-like over wooden frames. Beneath the tubes are resonators in the form of open-topped tin cans, sized appropriately to reinforce the tones of the tubes above.

Down at the low end of the pitch range, Old Granddad has large rectangular slabs of aluminum played like marimba bars, set over air-column resonators made of large-diameter tin cans stacked and soldered together, opened at the ends but for the very bottom. Old Granddad also includes six huge bells made of oxygen tanks with the bottoms sawed off, played by striking with baseball bats. The set is rounded out with ranch triangles, carefully selected garbage cans to be played as drums, and a few other sounding elements. Don't be misled by the commonplace and scrap materials in the instruments: the sound, reflecting careful thought and workmanship, is in every way refined and lovely. Countless other instrument makers — especially those interested in making something as de-

"CHERISH, CONSERVE, CONSIDER, CREATE"

LOU HARRISON

pendably tunable as it is sweet-sounding—have since taken advantage of these simple and affordable ideas.

Bill has gone on to build many more instruments, including flutes and a wonderful variety of strings and percussion. Lou has continued to play an interactive role in the instrument-design process, and assisted in the building and decorative work. Lou has also carefully worked out the tunings for the instruments, adhering closely to tenets of just intonation. Bill, for his part, has become the tuning technician. Eschewing stroboscopes and quartz tuners — standard tools of the tuner's trade — Bill has worked extensively with oscilloscopes to observe wave forms and frequency relationships. He has also built exquisitely accurate *monochords* (simple one - or two-string zithers designed for the study of pitch relationships, carefully calibrated over their string lengths to facilitate pitch comparisons).

Since the construction of Old Granddad around 1970, the idea of an American music taking inspiration from the music of Java and Bali has developed into what has been called "the American Gamelan movement." The movement has given rise to a lot of wonderful music from many different composers and performance groups, some of it carefully modeled after Indonesian music and some of it thoroughly American in style. A central part of the movement has been the construction of new instruments in search of gamelan-inspired sounds. Composers and builders alike have gone about their work with a bow of respect and thanks to Bill Colvig and Lou Harrison.

(A final note: in the last few years Old Granddad had begun to show signs of age. At Lou and Bill's invitation, the instruments have now been reconstructed from scratch by the fine instrument maker Richard Cooke of Utah.) ✦

ARTHEA

KOTAR, CONTRABASS NEY, TUBE GONGS AND MORE

The members of Arthea make every part of every instrument they use. "We are," says François Bourlier, "the slave of the instruments."

Goa Alloro and François Bourlier first met in 1967. They shared an interest in music from around the world, and along with a group of other musicians, they took to presenting performances with a tremendous array of instruments. François and Goa quickly recognized that the mix-and-match approach had its drawbacks. Each of the diverse instruments they were bringing together, they came to understand, was dependent in its musical functioning upon its own cul-tural context. In addition to problems of balance and tuning, there were questions with regard to musical and cultural mean-ing. So Goa and François began to develop an idea for creating instruments of their own. The instruments would be designed to work together in ensemble, establishing their own musical habitat and, with it, a world of musical possibili-ties. Yet they would be seen not as new inventions, but as natural descendents of the varied instruments that the group members so loved.

Goa and François formed a new group under the name Arthea, committed to the idea of playing instruments of their own making. Goa took on the work of master craftsman, with assistance from François in both conceptualization and execution. "Goa can build castles; he can build boats; he can build planes; he can fix the plumbing in your house; every-thing," says François. "If he doesn't have the tools he needs, he builds the tools."

And so Arthea began building instru-ments — a whole new ensemble's worth of them. The work has continued ever

Members of Arthea in their workshop

Arthea's Salon of Music

since. Many of them have been stringed instruments, influenced by prototypes from throughout the Asian continent. The *Kotar*, for instance, is a zither-like instrument. It has movable upright A-shaped bridges set mid-string like the Japanese *koto*, as well as the overtone-enhancing buzzing bridge of some of the stringed instruments of India, with further influences from the Chinese *qin* and the Persian *tar*.

Perhaps the most visually striking of Arthea's instruments is a wind instrument: the *Contrabass Ney*. It is one of a family of flutes that Goa has made in homage to the ney flute found throughout the Middle East. The contrabass ney is over ten feet long, constructed of brass with painstaking care and featuring a meticulously crafted keying system. A variety of percussion instruments appear among Arthea's instrumentarium as well, including frame drums, cymbals and gongs in various forms.

In addition to the workshop in which the instrument making takes place, Arthea maintains a separate recording studio and workshop equipped for sound analysis, including "an anechoic chamber where we measure and test." Research performed here feeds the instrument design and construction processes. But thirty years of experience allows the members of the group to blend hard-earned intuition with scientific data in the instrument-making work. Despite the analysis and extraordinary craftsmanship that goes into the making of the instruments, François speaks of the instruments primarily from a philosophical perspective. "What is important is to hear other musical civilizations," he says; "to hear the music, the rhythms, the melodies, and also the spirituality that the music is sounding with."

François also marvels at the ability of the music and the instruments to provide a gateway to the inner self. "If I have one lesson to get from all the work we do, it is that this music gives me a kind of key to understand something new and to be more open, to be more universal and to be less ... crazy, you know? If we make instruments, if we make beautiful music, it's an accident. What we want to work for is our soul." ✦

RICHARD JAMES (aka Aphex Twin)

COMPUTERS, SAMPLERS AND ELECTRONICS

Richard James' piece on this CD is called "Bucephalus Bouncing Ball," and it does indeed feature the sound of a bouncing ball. It's recognizable as a series of thumps that starts out slow and becomes more rapid, like a ball rebounding less with each bounce and gradually coming to rest. So here's a question: Is it a real bouncing ball sound that we hear, electronically sampled and inserted into the piece? Or is the effect a simulation, with values for the decreasing loudness and the diminishing time between each hit formulated in advance and programmed into some software

> **"MY TWO AMBITIONS ARE TO MAKE MUSIC FOREVER AND TO NEVER GET A JOB."**

subroutine? The person to answer that question, of course, is Richard himself — but he prefers not to discuss his methods.

To understand Richard James' music, it will help to understand a bit about the musical genres around which he works. In the U.S., Europe and beyond there is a world of urban dance music that for the most part evades over-30 radar screens. The world comes to life after-hours at clubs and warehouse parties and raves, where the key figure is a particularly evolved species of disk jockey. Working with turntables, mixers, computers, and other equipment, the DJ blends and processes sound sources (from records, CDs, computer files or, increasingly, live acoustic and electric sources) to create a dance-and-trance-inducing stream of beats and melodies. These musician/DJs become experts on the question of what tempos — how many beats-per-minute — will induce what sorts of physiological and psychological responses in the dancers. For the uninitiated, the com-

plaint is that there's nothing to DJ music but the beat, going on endlessly. For devotees, the beat is a river through which myriad musical elements flow.

Richard James has worked as a DJ since he was seventeen years old. And since well before that, he has been a maker of the music — the composer and master technician who creates the recordings from which the DJ works. In earlier days, he worked with various sorts of electronic equipment for making, manipulating and recording sounds. Very little of it was standard gear. In an abortive stint in a trade school electronics course, he learned to make circuit boards, and from there began building much of his own equipment from the bottom up. He also took to extensively modifying and rewiring off-the-shelf equipment that came his way. Speaking a few years ago of his homemades, he said "Some of them don't look like any-

I DON'T WANT SESSION MUSICIANS WITH A BRAIN. I JUST WANT ROBOT MUSICIANS WHO CAN TELL EXACTLY WHAT I WANT THEM TO DO."

thing else apart from boxes with knobs on them. Some maybe look like normal keyboards, but with all my things inside. I'm not into carpentry and stuff, so I use existing shells of other keyboards sometimes, and other times I just build them from scratch." Details as to the nature of the hardware within remain undisclosed. What is known is that the sounds that began turning up on his recordings were unlike anything that others working with standard gear were creating.

With the advent of digital technology, Richard also developed an extensive library of sampled sounds — that is, recorded sounds stored in digital format making them readily accessible for electronic manipulation. Steel girders and clanging pipes, sandpaper, vacuum cleaners and blenders, even (the story goes) the micro—sound of a beetle climbing into a tap — this is his raw material. By the time the sounds have gone through his electronic processing and reappeared in recorded works, their original identities are often entirely obscured.

Technology does not hold still. In recent years, the boxes with knobs on them have been replaced by computers — usually Macs, often used in multiples (Richard owns three of them). For the DJing jobs, departing from the traditional turntables, he now works from a laptop, using mostly tracks prepared in his home studio. The making of circuit boards has been replaced by the writing of software, and as with hardware, much of what he uses is customized by himself and like-minded programmers.

Richard James comes out of the world of dance music, and that is where his primary audience lies. Yet he himself acknowledges no influences — "It's like me and my music are totally isolated from anything," he says. The music, in his view, is entirely self-referential; he works his insomniac hours in a bedroom studio without the least regard for what others might make of his sounds. He regularly breaks the rules of the form to follow a vision entirely his own, and he's not always slave to the beat. For listeners not of the dance music world, that's good — it means that the logic of the music, as well as its pure, logic-defying inventiveness, are not specific to the genre. They're there to be savored by anyone willing to listen. ✦

LES PHÔNES

STILTOPHONES, PONGOPHONES AND MORE

Jean-Claude Charlier and Franck Pillonetto sat at a table one day — this was about a dozen years ago now — enjoying a conversation over a glass of wine. The talk turned to making music with wine glasses, and they started playing the glasses on the table. As they did, they were captured by certain characteristics of the sound. Played together, they found that the tones mingled in ways that made it impossible to know who was producing what sound. "...and the more we played," Franck Pillonetto recalls, "the more we had the impression that we could stop playing, and the music would go on."

It was this sort of thinking about music and sound — sound as a living thing to be cultivated by the players but not necessarily controlled — that gave rise to the group Les Phônes. Jean-Claude and Franck, later joined by Marianne Ponlot, have gone on to develop a number of instruments for the purpose of encouraging and exploring this kind of musical awareness.

Les Phônes' primary instrument, created over the last five years and still evolving, is *Stiltophones*. Stiltophones are literally stilts: two stick-like uprights with foot-ledges and hand-holds, upon which the player stands and dances. Each upright supports a pair of flutes, ranging in length up to about nine feet. The lower end of the stick is equipped with a spring-mounted pneumatic system, such that the player's weight, with each movement, pumps air across the sounding edges of the flutes. The

"WE DON'T CONSIDER OURSELVES MUSICIANS. WE ARE ONLY HUMAN BEINGS TRYING TO REALIZE THE HUMANITY INSIDE OF US WITH MUSIC."

Les Phônes

flutes have no toneholes; instead, they function as "harmonic flutes:" the air columns are long enough relative to diameter that they're easily made to sound one of the tube's harmonic overtones rather than the fundamental. They can produce clearly any of the first seven or eight tones in the harmonic series, depending on the strength of the player's movement and the resulting force of air, giving each flute a gamut of available tones despite the lack of toneholes. For the performer, Franck says, the playing is "a kind of dynamic weightlessness, because we are on springs."

Dancing on stilts might seem an odd approach to controlling musical sound; a far cry from, for instance, the facile action of keyboard playing. But in the stiltophones, Franck Pillonetto says, "we tried to make an instrument able to transform the movement of the whole body into music. An instrument we can control or be controlled by; an instrument we don't have to control with the mind alone, but with the body or soul too." Versions of the instrument currently

in development will have a bypass valve. This will allow the option of intermittent silence as the dancing continues, to create a kind of subtractive music that Franck likens to the stone sculptor revealing the form by removing material rather than adding.

When they are up on the stiltophones and moving in rhythm, the members of Les Phônes fall into a thoroughly engaged, closely interlocking music, hypnotic in its effect on players and listeners alike. You can hear this in the second part of Les Phônes' track on the accompanying CD.

The first part of the track shows another of the Les Phônes instruments, the *Pongophone*. It is an arrangement of vibrating plates, similar to a xylophone or vibraphone, but in this case with plates of glass (another version of the instrument uses aluminum). They are set very close alongside one another to form a flat, uniform, table-like surface about three-feet wide by six-feet long. It is used, in fact, as a ping pong table. Two players can rally in the usual fashion, with the ball pinging and ponging musically as it chances to strike here and there among the differently-pitched plates.

The players can also expand the possibilities: "Sometimes we play ping pong with many balls, and we play the plates with the fingers at the same time, to mix conscious rhythm and random rhythm." The pongophone shows the group's lighter side, but it also carries a message about how we interact with sound: in the randomness of the ping pong game is an opportunity for the players to partake in the sound, and to enjoy it, without seeking entirely to control it.

The members of Les Phônes have created other instruments — *Anthémophones*, *Héliophones*, *Granopluviophones* and more — but the stiltophones remain their primary focus. They compare the stiltophone to a seemingly very different instrument: the Australian *didjeridu*. It, too, Franck notes, converts movement into music. "For the didjeridu, it's based on very deep inner movement: breath. For the stiltophones it's based on the very 'deep outside' movement of the body, like in a walk or in a dance. But this is also a very deep inside movement, almost automatic, like breath. A movement you don't have to think about to do perfectly. A movement you can control or be controlled by."

"Music," he continues, "is not a matter of making a form. We don't believe that the musician has to transform the sound to make it into the form he wants. We believe that the musician has to transform himself with the sound. When we make music we don't want to organize it; we want to taste it, to discover it and to arrive when we're finished playing in place where we have never gone before." ✦

Les Phônes' Stiltophones

PETER WHITEHEAD

NEW FOLK INSTRUMENTS

The first time I saw Peter Whitehead perform, he used a plastic bag filled with some kind of small, rattley things — shells or pebbles, perhaps. In a kneeling position, he repeatedly lifted the sack and let it fall back to the wooden floor, producing a simple rhythm to accompany his singing. There was more to the performance than this, of course, but I mention the rattle-sack because of its evocative simplicity. It's a far cry from the more elaborate music you'll hear from Peter on the CD that accompanies this book, but it is emblematic of his approach to sound-making.

"In some ways," says Peter, "I think of what a lot of us do as a modern kind of folk art." Peter makes musical instruments mainly with commonplace materials — cookie tins, cooking utensils, scrap wood, bobby pins, balloons. "I tend to work from things that I can find around me. I don't have any schooling in music, so I tend to do things by instinct. I'm not working within a framework where I know what kind of music I'm expected to play or what kind of instruments I'm expected to make, and that, to me, is folk music."

What kind of instruments does Peter Whitehead make? Lately he's been making lots of string instruments — lute-like things and lyres, both plucked and bowed. The resonators for these are typically made from pans or tins or other sorts of household containers. Metal soundboards often give them a distinctive sound. Most of the bowed strings are in the style of Asian spike fiddles such as the Chinese *erhu*, with relatively small bodies and a cylindrical neck. These are played not by fingering the strings against a fingerboard to control the pitch, but rather by pressing the string mid-air — a technique affording greater flexibility and a high degree of expressiveness, but more demanding in terms of intonation. Many of the stringed

Peter Whitehead playing the Lawn Lyre

instruments are made to accent the high overtones within the sound, through the use of buzzing bridges, special bowing techniques and the like.

For wind instruments, Peter has made several large *harmonics flutes* — that is, flutes without finger holes which produce tones of the harmonic series. He also works with the peculiar wind-sound arrangement sometimes called a membrane reed — a unique system in which a membrane stretched over the end of the tube serves the same function as the reed on a clarinet, allowing the air to enter in rapid pulses to create the vibration. Peter has made some extraordinary looking and sounding wind instruments this way, some with bagpipe-like arrangements of

drone and melody pipes, and some nvolving big, separate air chambers into which the instrument is played to greatly expand the resonance.

Peter's particular genius also comes out in the percussion instruments, where again he demonstrates a taste for adding rattles and buzzes to tones that would otherwise be simpler, purer, less interesting. For instance, consider the sound of a very long metal bar, mounted so as to vibrate when struck in a clear, long-sustaining tone. Now consider the effect of a tiny nail or pin dangled from a thread so that it dances, just touching, on the surface of the bar. It limns the tone with a silvery glitter. When the player moves the pin along the surface, crossing the nodes and anti-

Peter Whitehead playing the Spoon Harp

nodes of the bar's vibration pattern, the shimmering tone shifts delicately.

In other percussion constructions, Peter uses cans and springs and bicycle spokes and sheet metal. "I'm trying to assemble some kind of orchestra," he says. "So I investigate all the different sounds — low sounds, high sounds, percussion, strings ..." Some of his instruments are designed to fill a tonal gap in his sound palette, but as he comments, you don't always know when you set out to make an instrument what the outcome will be. As often as not, the actual results, and the musical possibilities they suggest, prove to be at least as interesting as anything you might have imagined beforehand.

Learning to play the instruments (remember, they don't come with instruction books) is a matter of starting from scratch, doing a lot of improvising, and exploring those possibilities. "Many of the instruments," Peter says, "are meant to be played with an instinctive sense — you have to feel them rather than know a lot of technique. For this reason a begin-ner can get in touch with the instruments' innate musicality fairly directly, without being blocked by a need for training."

Asked about the spirit that motivates his instrument making, Peter mentions several themes. He speaks of trying to find an authentic voice — a way of making music that is one's own, regardless of fashion. He speaks of feeling a sense of continuity with instrument makers since the beginning of time. He speaks of an inborn urge to make things with his hands. He speaks of the social aspect of music; of how people interact with it and within it; of how directly a musical instrument, made and shared and exchanged, will engage people. And as important as anything, he adds, is a spirit of playfulness. ✦

the Spoon Harp

51

ELA LAMBLIN

SCULPTAURALS

Soundcycle

E la Lamblin makes playable sound sculptures. The most ambitious of them are big, structural things that engage the musician in a kind of dance. Not the tiny dance of fingers on a key-board, but a full-bodied, room-filling sort of movement, acrobatic and athletic. This reflects an abiding interest in the choreo-graphic aspects of music making, and in music performance as theater.

Consider, for example, Ela's *Orbitone*. The orbitone is like a playground swing set — a big triangular frame with the equivalent of the child's swing hanging from the upper cross piece. But in place of the swing seat is a bar on which a per-son can stand, and the suspension chains are not chains, but rigid steel. Why rigid? Because this enables the swinger to do what he or she could never do as a child — swing higher and higher, and finally up and over and all the way around. The support beam above turns with the swing, and in so doing causes wheels to turn — bicycle-like wheels attached to the frame, and connected to the main bar by chain drive mechanisms. The wheels are fitted with sound devices around the rims, and the turning motion causes them to sound in various ways.

The orbitone developed as an off-shoot to Ela's earlier work with simple

Bell Wheels — bicycle wheels with spokes tuned by adjustment of their tensions, and with sounding objects such as telephone bells mounted around the perimeter with the rims facing outward. As the wheel turned, the tuned spokes could be played with light sticks, and the bells by percussion or a bow on the rims. Since the wheel provided the motion, the bow or striker could be stationary, stroking the bells as they passed. This led Ela to the idea of making a holder that could position bows or clappers against the bells for sound, or away from them for times of silence, leaving the player free to do other things.

The *Bell Wheels* idea led to other instruments as well, such as the *Sound Cycle*. Ela has described it as "a five-wheeled object," but it might help to think of it as a sort of tricycle-plus-two, with three wheels rolling on the ground and two more as sounding wheels turning above. A rider powers it with foot pedals (one of the three rolling wheels serves as both a drive wheel and a steering wheel), while attached chain-drives set the sound wheels above in motion. Bows and clappers, positioned to contact the bells as they pass, can be engaged for contact or no-contact. There are also canisters with tuned metal prongs extending outward all around; these too are set in rotational motion by chains and sprockets, and the prongs are plucked, kalimba-like, as they pass by carefully positioned plectra.

> **"I INVENT INSTRUMENTS BY FIRST CREATING A SCULPTURAL FORM, AND THEN FIGURING OUT WHICH SOUND IT WANTS TO MAKE."**

The waterfall tones of Bell Wheels can be heard throughout Ela's piece *"Cosmogenesis"* on the accompanying CD. For this recording, he removed the sound wheels from the Orbitone and the Sound Cycle and played them by hand in the studio.

Toward the end of "Cosmogenesis," you can hear another of Ela's instruments, the *Stamenphone*. The Stamenphone is a bowed-string instrument — albeit a bowed string instrument like no other. It doesn't share the semi-automatic approach of the orbitone and sound cycle. Instead, the player plays directly on the strings to create rhythm and melody. The stamenphone is an upright metallic structure, about six feet tall and two feet in diameter at its broadest, with sixteen strings of piano wire stretched from a cast bronze top and extending down to a stainless steel globe below. The globe serves as a resonator for the string sounds. A bit of water is kept in it, so that the sloshing within causes shifting resonances in the globe, giving the tone an ever-varying, iridescent quality. Ela sounds the strings by bowing, playing them entirely in harmonics: by touching the strings lightly at key points with one hand while bowing with the other, he can

Ela Lamblin playing the Stamenphone

54

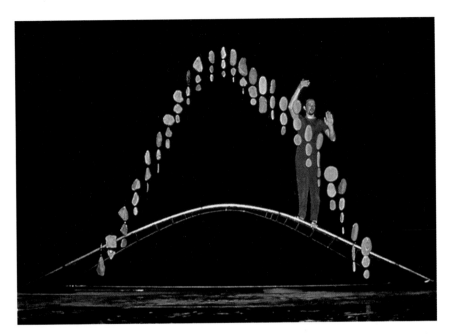

Ela Lamblin playing the Sine Stones

selectively bring out specific overtones, making an array of tones available from each string. "I took the image for the shape of it from a dream I had," Ela says, "in which I was playing a musical plant."

For theatrical performances, the stamenphone can become the *Aerial Stamenphone*. The instrument is suspended from the ceiling, with the player suspended as well, but separately,

55

so that the playing becomes an interaction of two independently swinging things, player and instrument.

Another instrument is the *Sine Stones*. This is a set of river rocks suspended by music wire from wooden sound boxes installed in the ceiling. The rocks serve as weights, providing tension on the strings, and the strings are played by rubbing them with rosined gloves to create a friction vibration. With the weight of the stones providing the necessary tension, the strings are tuned primarily by length. Given a high enough ceiling in the performance space, the strings are fairly long, and the rosined stroking technique creates longitudinal vibra-

The Orbitone

tions (see the chapter on Ellen Fullman's Long String Instrument). This kind of vibrating system sets up very strong harmonics, and Ela can bring out different harmonics by stroking the strings at different points along their lengths.

If all this sounds grand and theatrical, there's also a light and whimsical side to much of what Ela does. His *Carrot Flutes* may exist only as long as appetite allows, but they produce an amazingly clear tone while they last. His bamboo *Toe Flute*, with its warm, pentatonic bass flute sound, is played with the thumbs of each hand, arms extended as far as they can reach, while for the notes still farther down the tube the player uses his two big toes. *Jar Drums* with balloon rubber membranes, *Kelp Flutes* and saxophones, and hoop-shaped metal rainsticks help round out the collection.

Ela credits his creativity to his upbringing. He was home-schooled in a rural setting by parents who found the right balance of discipline and freedom for him. When he was a child, he recalls, his father made this agreement with

him: he would buy no toys for the boy, but he would help him to make anything he wanted. In that spirit, Ela is still making things. ✦

Bellwheels

JOHN CAGE

PREPARED PIANO

John Cage (1912-1992) was not primarily an instrument maker. His main interest lay in the existing sounds of the world around him, and only to a lesser extent in fabricating new sound-making devices. Yet his experiments with different sorts of sound-tools made a lot of waves, while, more significantly, his ways of thinking about sound, and non-sound too, profoundly affected several generations of the avant-garde.

Cage's earliest compositions employed conventional instruments played in a conventional manner, while the organizing principles of the music, reflecting the influence of serialism and other logical approaches, were more adventuresome. In the 1930s he began to work with pure percussion, assembling for his working ensemble a mostly metallic instrumentarium made up of brake drums, pots and bowls, bells, metal bars, sheets of tin and the like. One of his ideas from this time was the water gong — a gong to be dipped in water immediately after striking, causing its pitch to bend variably downward according to the depth of the dipping.

It was in 1940 that he first developed the instrument for which he is best remembered, the *Prepared Piano*. This is a grand piano which has been altered by the insertion of various items between the strings — nuts and bolts, bits of rubber and the like. The effect is to drastically alter the sound of the piano. According to the nature of the preparations — that is, what's inserted where — some of the notes may come out as percussive thunks or taps, while others are transformed into glittering gong-like timbres of infinite variability. "An instrument having convincingly its own special characteristics, not even suggesting those of a

"I LOVE SOUNDS, AND I ACTUALLY LOVE THEM MORE THAN WHAT WE'VE DONE TO THEM."

John Cage

piano," Cage said, "must be the result."

Different preparations can produce very different effects. "Just as you go to the beach and pick up pretty shells that please you," he once remarked, "I go to the piano and find sounds I like." Observers have often compared the sound of the prepared piano to that of the Indonesian gamelan, and inferred that this was what Cage was after. He downplayed this, saying that what he was really after was the huge practicality and convenience of having an entire percussion orchestra under the ten fingers of a single player. Even this doesn't describe it though. The sounds that arise are unlike any percussion orchestra on earth, because of the unique timbres and also because of the particular character of the musical lines that a pianistic playing technique brings forth.

Through the 1940s, Cage focused on prepared piano as his primary medium. This culminated in the major work, *Sonatas and Interludes for Prepared Piano*, premiered in 1949. In 1950, it was recorded with Maro Ajemian at the piano under Cage's direction. On the CD we have included "Sonata XIV" from this first recording as our example, chosen in part because it shows off so nicely the delicious timbres of the preparations.

In the years before and after his prepared piano work, Cage made music with many other sound sources and approaches to sound-making. During one period, he used contact mics to explore facets of microsonics, such as the tiny sounds of plucked cactus spines. He used record player cartridges somewhat similarly at one stage, inserting small objects into the cartridge and plucking or scraping them. He wrote a number of pieces for toy piano. For one of his major works, he used various pieces of equipment found in the early recording studio, including test records and oscillators. His latter days, completing the circle, saw him returning to standard orchestral instruments, bringing fresh ears to the flute and violin.

> **"WHICH IS MORE MUSICAL, A TRUCK PASSING BY A FACTORY OR A TRUCK PASSING BY A MUSIC SCHOOL?"**

John Cage's strongest legacy may lie as much in his ideas and personality as in his music itself. He was by nature a philosopher, and also a liver and lover of life. Music served as an arena in which he could work out and model some of his ideas. Those ideas were many and diverse; all interlinked; often embedded in zen-like paradox; frequently surprising, and at the same time, surprisingly obvious. Cage did not feel that music should be about individual self-expression, or about the artist trying to create some-

thing grand and beautiful. He felt that music should be revelatory rather than expressive, and revelatory in an entirely transparent way: it should allow the listener to become aware of what was already there. "Everything we come across," as he once remarked, "is to the point." ✦

The Prepared Piano

STOMP

EVERYTHING

Each chapter in this book has a title consisting of the names of the artists or builders followed by the instruments they make or play. This chapter is called "Stomp: Everything," because everything is what the Stomp people play.

Stomp is a theater piece built around a group of performers who create irresistibly rhythmic music — and irresistibly rhythmic dance — using commonplace objects as their noise makers. There is no real plot, and there is no dialog. In the show's opening number, a performer enters the stage with a push broom. He begins to sweep. Another sweeper soon appears, and another, and as they set about tidying up their respective areas of the stage, seemingly oblivious to one another, the sweeping sounds begin to take on a rhythmic quality. Soon enough the swishing and knocking of the brooms has evolved into one great, danceable, interlocking groove, and the show is on its way. With each new segment, the players appear on stage with another unassuming object which soon reveals a hidden musicality.

One piece involves the igniting of Zippo lighters; another the scrunching of plastic bags. In one, players come forward with fully functional kitchen sinks strapped over their shoulders, and proceed to explore the musical potential of doing the dishes. In one of the showiest numbers the players perform a loud, over-sized dance with 50-gallon oil drums strapped to their feet like giant platform shoes. The audience grasps the idea immediately — there's sound and rhythm in everything — and with a zillion unexpected answers to the question "What next?" the game never gets old.

> **"STOMP IS THE EXPLORATION OF RHYTHM IN EVERYDAY THINGS."**

Stomp began in 1991 as the brainchild of Luke Cresswell and Steve McNicholas. The two were longtime collaborators, having started as buskers in their native Brighton a decade before, and moved on to several TV, film and theater music projects. *Stomp* opened in London and Edinburgh and, on a wave of critical success that followed, toured several continents with the original British cast. When the show found a second home in New York City, a new

American cast was created, allowing the original troupe to return to the U.K. Since then more casts have come into being: as of this writing there are five. Luke and Steve continue as the guiding force, although they are quick to point out that they leave plenty of room for each group to develop its own character. The show continues to evolve today, with new numbers being added or old ones reworked on a regular basis.

> "EACH PERFORMER HAS TO CREATE A CHARACTER THAT LIVES AND BREATHES IN THE STOMP WORLD, WHERE RHYTHM IS THE ONLY LANGUAGE."

Commercial recordings of the music from Stomp's stage show have not been made available. "We don't want to do it until we feel that we can create a journey through sound," Steve says, "in the same way that the show is a journey through sound." Recordings of Stomp are thus a rarity, and we're proud to be able to present one here on the accompanying CD. The piece, "Waterphonics," is taken from the sound track to *Stomp Out Loud*, a TV special recently produced by HBO. "It's something we've wanted to do for a long time," Steve says of the piece. "We've wanted to incorporate chimes and water into the show, and we've found it impossible."

What was not feasible on stage, however, was feasible for filming on location. Members of the New York cast found their way to an old pier, part of a former flour factory in Red Hook, Brooklyn. "The business had died," Steve recalls. "It's all derelict now; the pier's half collapsed." At a loading bay at the base of the pier was a "beautiful pool, just the perfect size, and the way the sunlight hit it at a certain time of day, it just glowed an emerald green." To set up for the piece, lengths of copper tubing were suspended by stretchy rubber cord from the rafters above, so that the tube ends just dipped into the water.

The Stomp players stood in the water, on a metal grid set three feet below the surface. When the chimes were struck, their shifting positions in the water caused the pitch to bend and wob-

Stomp playing newspapers

ble. The players used a special technique, pulling the copper tube into the water, then striking it just after releasing it. As it sprung back upward on the cord, the player damped the sound by catching it — all with perfect rhythmic precision. The instruments also included a selection of metal bowls, played half-submerged for a characteristic wobbly tone. Stomp's philosophy in making the HBO special was that it should be in the spirit of live performance rather studio re-creation, and so what you hear on this CD is very much a real-time affair.

Steve McNicholas cites vintage Hollywood musicals as a prime influence for *Stomp*, as well as more native influences. "In Britain there's a kind of Vaudevillian tradition which is very eccentric and idiosyncratic." He mentions Spike Milligan, "kind of the Godfather of surreal comedy in Britain." Milligan pranced about on stage with all sorts of unlikely props, and often turned his shenanigans, one way or another, into music. There's a certain British blue-collar feeling in *Stomp*, showing itself in the performers' dress, in the occupations of the characters depicted, in something about the style of the visual humor. There's no particular message in this, Steve says; it's simply a reflection of the creators' backgrounds; a matter of "where we come from and who we are" that informs the show.

"Ultimately, all we're doing is having a lot of fun with rhythm," he concludes. "Who hasn't, in a restaurant — maybe only when they were a kid — picked up a fork and played out a tune on a row of glasses. The impulse to do that — that's what the show is about, really, and that's what it hooks into." ✦

SHARON ROWELL

HUACA

I t was close to twenty years ago, when Sharon Rowell was living in the California coastal town of Mendocino, that she found herself falling in love with the sound of an offshore foghorn. "It had this beautiful, deep sound. It was very intimate; it wasn't like these blasting fog horns in San Francisco bay. It seemed like it was speaking just to me, and I wanted to answer that foghorn." Sharon's beautifully formed musical instrument, the *Huaca*, is a response to that call.

The *Huaca* is a triple-chambered vessel flute. In vessel flutes, the instrument body is not long and thin and tubular, but fatter in shape. The old fashioned "sweet potato" *ocarina* is an example; so is the cider jug of the traditional jug band. Vessel flutes are similar to tubular flutes in many ways: the sound is produced by an air stream striking an edge, and they can employ finger holes to produce a range of notes. But vessel flute tone tends to be rounder and warmer, perhaps "hootier," having almost no overtone content. Most ocarina-like instruments, including Sharon's, are fipple flutes, meaning that they employ an air duct, like that of a recorder, to direct the air-stream to the sounding edge.

Sharon makes her triple flutes of clay, using firing techniques that give them a warm and earthy look even while the shapes themselves are models of proportion, elegance and simplicity. In most of the instruments the three chambers are all the same size, ranging from about three inches in diameter in the smaller, higher-pitched instruments to about six in the big, low-toned ones. Typically, the two front chambers are identical, having four or five finger holes. With various

combinations of covered and uncovered holes, this gives them a range of something over an octave. The rear chamber in many of the instruments is a drone, having no finger holes and producing a single tone. In others it may have one or two holes, playable by the palms of the hands. The three chambers are connected to a single mouthpiece, often with two ducts — one leading to the two front vessels, and one to the drone. By blowing only into the upper duct, the player can choose to play the melody chambers without the drone.

Sharon Rowell and Alan Tower

Two Huacas

On seeing Sharon's instruments, one's first thoughts might be about the intricate, contrapuntal music a skilled player could make with three flutes in one. And indeed, many players have done beautiful things along these lines. But the loveliest qualities of the huacas come forth in the simplest music. When the two melody chambers play a single line in unison, there arises a chorusing effect of inexpressible beauty. The effect can be heard by listeners in the room, and you get some sense of it in recordings as well. But it is most present for the player. With the melody chambers on each side, close to the player's ears, the sound becomes three dimensional and enveloping; it seems to come from nowhere and everywhere. And so, while the huaca can be a most effective instrument in performance, it really finds it place as a personal instrument — a meditation instrument, one to take to someplace quiet and play by oneself.

Sharon is conscious of her role as innovator. At the same time, she feels a connection to the centuries-old practice of traditional clay ocarina making. "The ocarina is such a beautiful, beautiful instrument," she says. "I feel privileged to be part of the historical continuity of it ... in a very small way, like a grain of sand on the beach."

The huaca piece on the accompanying CD, "Elegy for the Missing," is performed by the instrument's most advanced player, Alan Tower. Alan's music

"THE SOUND OF AN OCARINA — THE VERY FIRST SOUND IT MAKES WHEN IT'S STILL WET, WHEN YOU'RE FORMING IT — IS, TO ME, JUST A MAGICAL EVENT."

is often contrapuntal and complex. ("Alan has mastered this instrument," says Sharon.) Over the years he has worked closely with Sharon in the creation of made-to-order instruments for his performances, including huacas with extended ranges and huacas in multiple keys. He too, sees in the instrument a invitation to secluded meditation; he also works to bring it to a wider audience in performances and recordings. ✦

BRADFORD REED

THE PENCILINA

Bradford Reed plays his instrument, the *Pencilina*, in the streets of New York. "I've been to court," he says; "I've had people yell at me: 'You vagabond! Get out from in front of my place!'" He's concerned that opportunities for street musicians have diminished in the city in recent years, and worries about how "municipal politics come into play" as regards the use of public space. But he continues to do it because it's fun; it fits his temperament; his

musical style is suited to outdoor presentation; and most people really dig the music when they hear it.

The pencilina is an electric board zither played primarily by striking the strings with sticks; also by plucking and bowing. Bradford first created it around 1985, and has continued to refine it. ("It just keeps developing," he says.) The basic form is of two boards mounted parallel to each other on a stand, like extended guitar necks with no bodies. Each has a bridge at either end, and tuning machines at one end. One of the necks has six guitar strings stretched across it; the other has four bass strings. Wedged over and under the strings in each neck is a stick — an old drum stick for the guitar strings and a metal rod for the bass strings. The sticks divide each string into two segments, one on each side, which vibrate quasi-independently and so can be played separately. The sticks can also be moved to alter the effective string lengths on either side.

There are four built-in pickups: two are contact mics mounted in the bridges at one end of each neck, and two are guitar-style electromagnetic pickups which are placed under the strings toward the opposite end. In addition, there are four bells — a fire bell, a door bell, and two brass telephone ringer bells — mounted at the end of one of the necks. The contact mics pick up the ringing of the bells through the wood of the instrument. They also pick up percussion anywhere else on the wooden necks, so any spot that happens to produce a nice sound is available for drumming.

The slidable stick arrangement, it turns out, is laden with odd sound possibilities. Typically the wedged stick divides each string into two separate string segments with different pitches depending on their relative lengths. But for many stick locations, there is communication across the stick, so that when one side is struck the segments on both sides contribute to the sound. The quality of this effect depends on the pitch relationship between the two strings segments and whether they share any overtones frequencies in common. All manner of strange gong-tones can arise, infinite in their variability. Other special effects occur when the player pivots or flexes the wedged sticks to change the tension on the strings as they sound. The fact that the electromagnetic pickups are movable adds yet another parameter.

The instrument, as you may guess, is completely idiosyncratic — and yet within its idiosyncrasy lies a world of possibilities. Bradford's phrase is "I haven't hit a wall with it yet" — meaning that in all the years he's been playing, he hasn't exhausted any facet of its potential. "It's been my primary focus for a long time, and I'm still learning and trying to improve on it. I've grown to really like what the pencilina can do."

Bradford currently uses a pair of shortened timbale sticks to strike the strings. But yes — when first he began to play the instrument, he used a pair of pencils as his strikers. ✦

"I WOULD GO ON AND MAKE OTHER INSTRUMENTS, BUT I HAVEN'T HIT A WALL WITH THE PENCILINA."

Bradford Reed and the Pencilina

ELLEN FULLMAN

THE LONG STRING INSTRUMENT

What, you may ask, is the reasoning behind this? Here in Ellen Fullman's *Long String Instrument*, are musical strings over one-hundred feet long. Doesn't such a drastic change of scale alter the physics of the sound-making process? Wouldn't strings thirty times the length of those on a standard bass produce frequencies so far below the human hearing range as to be musically useless?

Yes they would, if they were operating in the transverse mode of vibration. Transverse vibration is the mode by which stringed instruments normally produce their sound. It's the side-to-side movement that

you get when you pluck or bow across the strings. But other modes of vibration can occur as well. One of them is the longitudinal mode, which can be excited by stroking the string lengthwise. Here the vibration is a rapid forward-and-backward oscillation in the direction of the string's length, coming about as waves of compression reflect back and forth through the material of the strings. As with transverse vibration, the string can be attached to a soundboard at one end to project the vibratory movement out into the air so it can be heard.

But compression waves travel through the material of the string at extraordinarily high speeds — much higher than the analogous motion in transverse vibration. As a result, in the longitudinal mode it takes a much longer string to produce the same frequencies as a transversely vibrating guitar or violin or bass string. Therein lies the answer to the question, "Why so long?" Ellen Fullman's Long String Instrument, with strings vibrating in the longitudinal mode, requires lengths of 30, 60, 100 feet and more just to produce tones within the audible musical ranges.

Ellen Fullman and Nigel Jacobs playing The Long String Instrument

The Long String Instrument, in Ellen's hands, has taken many different forms over the years, and it continues to change according to the requirements of different musical purposes and installa- tion spaces. Still, a somewhat standard arrangement has taken shape. In it there are three banks of about twenty strings each, lined up alongside each other. Two of these are divided by double-sided

soundboards, so that in effect there are separate sets of strings extending from each side of the board. The far ends of the strings are anchored to the far walls of the installation space or whatever else can serve the purpose at a suitable distance. The third bank of strings comprises the bass strings; they run the entire length of the installation with a soundboard at one end, some suitable means of anchoring at the other, and no break along the length. Thus there are a total of four shorter string sets and one longer set, with about a hundred usable strings.

The instrument is normally played by three players. Two stand facing each other on opposite sides of the double-sided soundboards, in the alley between the two banks of strings. They can play by walking forward or backward, drawing their fingers (prepared with a rosin for better friction) along the strings on each side as they step. A third player is responsible for the long bass strings. An extensive array of harmonic overtones sound out within the tone as strongly as the underlying fundamental, and by stroking at different locations along the string the player can bring out different overtones selectively.

You can't tune the instrument by adjusting string tension — tension does not affect frequency in the longitudinal mode. The individual strings are tuned, instead, by adjusting the length of the main vibrating portion of the string. This, it turns out, is easy to do. All it takes to cause sufficient reflection in the compression wave is a sudden change in mass at some point along the string. That extra mass will define an end point for a standing wave, even if the wire extends beyond the location of the mass. Ellen achieves this simply by attaching C-clamps to the strings at the desired end points. Retuning is easy: just move the clamps.

Ellen first began to develop the Long String Instrument around 1981. She came upon on the stroked-strings idea initially by chance, and refined it over the years. The process has been essential to the development of her own musicality, both as creator and listener. The physics of the instrument, with its harmonic overtone structure measured out in the proportions and walking distances of the strings, have given her a special view into the ways of harmony and scale — a natural, physical perspective that students in a music theory course might

"THE MUSIC IS AN ARTIFACT LEFT OVER FROM THE JOURNEY."

never see. "I was an outsider to music," she says of the early days, "and it's as if now, through the instrument, I am seeing the inner workings, the gears, pulleys and bricks that build music... The project has become for me a personal music school. The instrument is like a microcosm of the history of music."

It is, by its nature, a walking instrument: an integral part of the music is the choreography of the players' movements along the strings. The playing technique is well suited to the long line. The slow, sweeping tones invite you not to listen for the march-by of rhythm and melody, but rather to follow the changing colors of sustained sounds and unhurriedly shifting harmonic relationships. At the same time, the long string instrument does have the potential for harmonic, melodic and rhythmic development on a more rapid time scale, and some of Ellen's more recent works reflect these qualities. For the accompanying CD, we've chosen an excerpt from her performance *Change of Direction*. Listen for the ways in which fountains of separate overtones arise from the sound of a single string. Then listen for the varicolored harmonies that develop from her careful tunings, as the overtones from different strings layer themselves upon one another.

"When I started this thing so many years ago," she says, "I was fascinated with the pedestrian aspect of it: that anyone could just touch it and walk, and it would make these sounds. But through the years I've found that that's not enough, and there are ways to touch it that sound more interesting than others. It's so responsive to pressure changes and speed; every body movement is reflected in the sound. It is a dance." ✦

UAKTI

FROM GRAM PAN TO AQUALUNG

Four Brazilian musicians make up the ensemble Uakti: Marco Antonio Guimaraes, Decio de Souza Ramos, Artur Andres Ribeiro and Paulo Sergio Santos. All of them are conservatory-trained, having first come together in the mid-1970s as members of the Minas Gerais State Symphony Orchestra, where Decio and Paulo were percussionists, Artur a flautist, and Marco a cellist. As classical musicians they held the work of Mozart, Stravinsky, Debussy and Villa Lobos in the highest regard — and,

indeed, they still do. But each was looking for a musical outlet with more freedom and self-determination than their symphonic work afforded.

Marco had begun making unconventional musical instruments, and the four started exploring their musical possibilities. They took the name "Uakti," after an Amazonian Indian folkloric figure: a beast with holes in its body who roamed the forests, the wind passing through its holes to create a strange and beautiful music. As Marco's instruments became increasingly refined and sophisticated, the players developed a distinctive musical style around them, and Uakti grew into an ensemble of unusual coherence and originality.

At the core of Uakti's instrumentarium is a family of three related instruments: the *Gram Pan*, the *Inclinated Pan*, and the *Trilobyte*. The "pan" in the names refers not to the Trinidadian steel drum, but to pan pipes. Like the traditional pipes of pan, the gram pan consists of a set of tubes mounted alongside one another, graduated in length from shortest and highest in pitch to longest and lowest. But the pipes of the gram pan are not hand-held. They are mounted in a stand for ease of playing, for the gram pan is a bass instrument of grand scale: the pipes are two or three inches in diameter, in lengths ranging up to about ten feet. They are played percussively on the open ends of the tubes with a specially designed large, soft, flat mallet, each stroke setting the air within into a brief but strong vibration. The sound is full and loud, exciting and rhythmic, but also clearly pitched and melodic.

In recent versions of the instrument, the last few feet of each pipe are made of a flexible tubing so that all the pipe ends can be positioned to terminate in the same place, opening from beneath into an open-topped box-like form. Bringing the ends together like this makes the microphone placement for recording or amplification much easier, and the box also imparts a bit more resonance to the sound.

The inclinated pan is the same instrument realized on a smaller scale to produce a higher register. The trilobyte differs from the two pans in that it has a skin, like a drumhead, over the playing ends of the tubes, giving it a different tone quality.

Uakti's instrumentarium also includes a marimba-like instrument with glass bars, and another with wooden bars. There are a variety of string instruments, including *The Tower* — a cylindrical, large-diameter tube with eleven strings stretched end to end, mounted so that it can rotate. "We had an accident," Artur Andres Ribeiro explains, "and the cello bow had been broken." This led to the idea of an angled bow on which the hairs can be slackened or tightened. The tightened bow plays just one or two strings at a time. Once slackened, the hairs can curve around the Tower's cylinder-mounted strings to play many at once. With different tuning of the strings, unusual musical effects become possible.

Another Uakti sound source — "this instrument is really special," says Artur — is the *Aqualung*. It is a water-sound

"WE HAD TO EXPERIMENT
IN A VERY HAND-MADE WAY."

Uatki

81

instrument, but one of controllable pitch and melody. A stream of water from an oversized bottle mounted six feet above is directed into an arrangement in which a smaller pipe fits within a larger one. The larger is stopped at the bottom, and has an overflow tube at a certain height in the side, so that the water level rises to that level and stabilizes there. The inner pipe is hand-held and can be dipped to varying heights in the larger. It is the resonance of the smaller pipe's air column above the level of the gurgling water line that determines the instrument's tone: the farther in it is dipped, the shorter is the remaining air column above, and the higher the pitch.

These are just a few of the Uakti instruments. They have in all well over a hundred in regular use, and more are being created all the time; as a practical matter they bring about forty with them for performance when they tour. Artur Andres Ribeiro emphasizes how, over the years, the players "had to experiment in a very hand-made way" with the instruments. They worked as a group, exploring and developing the techniques for playing them; drawing out the music that lies within them. "You have to dedicate time, because there is no one to teach how to play the gram pan or the trilobyte. The instruments have no history ... you have to work hard and find your own way." +

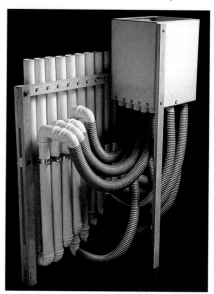

Gram Pan

LEONARD SOLOMON

THE MAJESTIC BELLOWPHONE

Leonard Solomon and the Majestic Bellowphone

Leonard Solomon's *Majestic Bellowphone* is a miracle of planning-as-you-go. No one but the person who oversaw the details of its development is likely to have the patience to learn to play it. But, oh, when the maker performs on the instrument of his making, what a wild delight!

"*The bellowphone,*" in Leonard's words, "is basically a random cluster of homemade organ pipes which are powered by squeeze balls." It's built entirely of salvaged materials, its thirteen pipes made variously of cardboard, aluminum, steel and brass. Some of the pipes are what organists call flute pipes — that is, they use a flute-like sounding principle —

and others are reed pipes. Leonard experimented with different sorts of reed and flute arrangements during the course of construction, with the result that there's no consistency of design: each pipe has its own characteristic sound and personality. Each requires a particular touch from the player ("part of the charm," Leonard notes).

Air is supplied to the pipes by various sorts and sizes of sports balls. Give one a squeeze, and air is directed through flexible tubings to the appropriate pipe or pipes. The balls mostly spring back to shape of their own volition, like a bulb horn. One exception is the big floor-mounted ball, played by one foot to control the lowest-pitched pipe, which depends on an externally mounted spring to help unsquash itself. A single pipe is reserved for mouthblowing via a connecting tube — good for a dramatic flourish at the end of a piece.

All of the pipes are tunable by various means, and they do often need a bit of tweaking due to changes in humidity or temperature. Asked if the pipes are tuned to a chromatic scale, Leonard replied "You'd never call it a chromatic instrument; it's more of an anarchic instrument." This is not to say that the pitches are random — in fact, the fine tuning must be rather carefully done, because, Leonard says, the instrument has the potential to sound really awful when it's out of tune. But the scale is not a complete chromatic scale. As with other features, the choice of available pitches developed gradually as the instrument took shape. "The first thing I made was just an oom-pah-pah ... and I just built everything around that initial oom-pah-pah in the key of D. Within the course of the several months that I was working on that, I would get all sorts of musical ideas for specific pieces that I thought would sound interesting on this machine, and so I would add pipes as I needed them."

If you've been listening to the bellowphone track on the accompanying

"MANY OF THE SERIOUS ALCHEMISTS OF HISTORY WERE ALSO MUSICIANS."

CD, you will by now be asking "How does he get all that music out of just thirteen pipes?" The answer is in the maze of balls, pipes and connectors that make up the bellowphone. To start, many of the pipes have side holes, open-and-closeable by means of levers or slides, which allow the single pipe to yield multiple pitches. In addition, some individual balls are hooked up to two or three pipes, so that squeezing one ball can produce a chord rather than a single tone. And these hook—ups are adjustable by various controls, so that, for instance, the chord that sounds for the ball in question can change to different chords from measure to measure within a performance.

Finally, the bellowphone is equipped with a wood block, a cowbell, two chimes and a taxi horn for added flavor. Leonard uses both hands and one foot to play the balls and control the various levers and sliders, and keeps a hammer in his right hand to sound the various percussion. At the same time he trades off on a kazoo and a nose flute held on a rack in front of him at mouth level. "It has taken a lot of practicing," he says.

Leonard also plays other instruments. The most important of these is another of his own making, the *Callioforte*. The Callioforte is basically a small organ of thirty-one chromatically tuned flute pipes. The bellows and air-feed mechanism are once again built around rubber balls — homemade ones in this case, made of liquid latex applied by brush over a form. It's a more orderly instrument, not as wildly idiosyncratic as the bellowphone. Still, it has its share of peculiarities. One is its unusual, though highly logical, keyboard layout, which for Leonard has now become more comfortable and natural than the standard keyboard. Beyond his unique instruments, there are other facets to Leonard's performances as well. He mentions juggling, and some sleight of hand and there's always a lot of humor. "It's basically entertainment," he says. "...heavy on the musical end." ✦

CREDITS

ABOUT THE AUTHOR

Bart Hopkin is a designer and builder of acoustic musical instruments, and a student of musical instruments worldwide. Since 1985 he has been publisher and editor of the quarterly journal *Experimental Musical Instruments*. He received a B.A. magna cum laude from Harvard University in folklore and mythology specializing in ethnomusicology in 1974, and later picked up a B.A. in music education and a teaching credential at San Francisco State University. He has taught extensively, composed, performed and recorded in various places and circumstances. In addition to his publications on musical instruments, he has researched and written on Jamaican children's songs (in the journal *Ethnomusicology*) and revival church music in Jamaica (*Jamaica Journal*). His book, *Making Simple Musical Instruments* was released by Lark Books in 1995. His *Musical Instrument Design, Practical Information for Instrument Making* was published by See Sharp Press in 1996, and the book-and-CD package *Gravikords, Whirlies and Pyrophones*, from Ellipsis Arts, also appeared in 1996. He now lives in Nicasio, California. ✦

RESOURCE GUIDE

Aphex Twin
Warp Records
Phone: 44-114-281-2000
Fax: 44-114-281-2002

Arthea
55, Route Napoleon 06130
Grasse, France
Phone: 33-4-93-36-51-04
Fax: 33-4-93-40-17-47
E-mail:
arthea.francois.bourlier@wanadoo.fr

Bill Colvig & Lou Harrison
New Albion Records
584 Castro St. #525
San Francisco, CA 94114
Phone: (415) 621-5757
Fax: (415) 621-4711
Email: ergo@newalbion.com
Website: http://www.newalbion.com

Ellen Fullman
P.O.Box 23347
Seattle, WA 98102
E-mail: efullman@eskimo.com

Bart Hopkin
Experimental Musical Instruments

Experimental Musical Instruments is a quarterly journal devoted to the design, construction and enjoyment of new and unusual musical instruments.

For information or a sample issue contact:
PO Box 784
Nicasio, CA 94946
Phone: (415) 662-2182
Fax: (415) 662-2182
E-mail: emi@windworld.com
Website: http://www.windworld.com/emi

Ela Lamblin
Lela Performance Group
711 37th Ave.
Seattle, WA 98122-5222
Phone: (206) 329-3724
Website: http://www.lela@CycoActive.com

Colin Offord
PO Box 279
Katoomba 2780, NSW Australia
Phone: 61-2-4784-1439
Fax: 61-2-4784-1439
Website:
http://www.artsitebluemountains.net.au

Les Phônes
26 A Rue St. Gilles 4000 Liège
Belgique
Phone: 32-4-223-0190
Fax: 32-4-223-0190

Bradford Reed
230 3rd St.
Brooklyn, NY 11215
Fax: (718) 403-7420
E-mail: Braf@earthlink.net
Website:http://www.home.earthlink.net/~braf

Sharon Rowell
Phone: (510) 524-7454
Alan Tower
226 18th Ave.
San Francisco, CA 94121
Phone: (415) 386-4334
Fax: (415) 502-5887
E-mail: Alantower@quickmail.ucsf.edu

Leonard Solomon
498 Old Bedford Rd.
Concord MA 01742
Phone: (978) 369-9951

ACKNOWLEDGEMENTS

Many people provided generous behind-the-scenes assistance to help pull this project together. The author sends a very big wide thank you to all of them, including:

Stanislav Avzan, Kathleen Brennan, Mitchell Clark, Chris Cutler, William Duckworth, Greg Eden, Charles Hanson, Laura Kuhn and the John Cage Trust, Margaret Leng Tan, Wendy Motchan, Foster Reed, Rachel Thomas, Jim Tremaine, and Don Wherry.

Stomp
Website:
http://www.usinteractive.com/stomp

Uakti Oficina Instrumental
Rua Rio Claro 37 Prado
Belo Horizonte Minas Gerais Brazil
Phone: 55-31-2914641
Fax: 55-31-2924211
E-mail: Uakti@metalink.com.br

Peter Whitehead
455 A Velencia St.
San Francisco, CA 94103
E-mail: linton@aol.com
Website:http://www.healthyarts.com/strat

ZGA
c/o ReR Megacorp
79 Beulah Rd. Thornton Heath,
Surrey CR7 8JG U.K.
E-mail: zga@sparc.spb.su
Website: http://www.sparc.spb.su/avz/zga/

PHOTO CREDITS

TRACK LISTINGS

TRACK LISTINGS

1. ZGA

Back to the East (4:23)
From the CD *ZGA: Sub Luna Morrior*
Chris Cutler at ReR Megacorp,
Recorded by M. Shemarov at MM Studios, St. Petersburg
℗ 1995 ReR

2. Colin Offord

Heavenly Flower (4:05) excerpt
From the CD Bow
P 1997 Colin Offord/Spiralsound, AMCOS

3. Tom Waits

Babbachichuija (2:18)
C Jalma Music / Lionel Conway L.A.
Recorded by Oz Fritz and Tim Ginnert, Prairie Sun Recording
℗ 1998 Tom Waits, ASCAP

4. Bill Colvig & Lou Harrison

Jhala III (2:00)
from Suite for Violin and American Gamelan
composed by Lou Harrison
from the CD *La Koro Sutro*
℗ 1988 New Albion Records

5. Arthea

Pentatonic (4:20)
From the CD *Passages*
℗ 1997 Wergo, SACEM

6. Aphex Twin

Bucephalus Bouncing Ball (5:45)
From the CD *Come to Daddy*
℗ 1997 Warp Records

7. Les Phônes

La Dance des Fourmis excerpt **and Megalithe (4:12)**
From the CD's *Mythes et légendes Phônes and Les Phônes Live 97*
Recorded by Benoit Dellerk
℗ 1995 Les Phones

8. Peter Whitehead

Tunnel of Love and **dear 3 (4:40)**
From the CD *Three Bags Full*
Recorded at Strange Attractor Studio
℗ 1997 Peter Whitehead, BMI

9. Ela Lamblin

Cosmogenesis excerpt **(4:54)**
From the CD *Sculptaural*
Recorded by Tom Stiles, Jack Straw Studio
Ⓟ 1996 Ela Lamblin

10. John Cage

Sonata XIV (3:31)
from Suites and Interludes for Prepared Piano
Performed by Maro Ajemian
From the CD *John Cage Sonatas and Interludes for Prepared Piano*
Henmar Press, ASCAP
Recorded by Douglas Hawkins, WOR Studios NYC
Ⓟ 1995 Composers Recordings Inc.

11. Stomp

Waterphonics (2:20)
Excerpt from the HBO video *Stomp Out Loud*
Ⓟ 1997 Stomp

12. Sharon Rowell

Elegy for The Missing (3:56)
Composed and performed by Alan Tower
Eclectic Music
A Mingled Destinies Production
Recorded by Evolution Sound
Ⓟ 1998 Alan Tower

13. Bradford Reed

Motivational Music for Pedetrians (4:22)
From the CD *Bradford Reed - Live at Home*
Ⓟ 1996 Bradford Reed, BMI

14. Ellen Fullman

Change of Direction excerpt **(4:52)**
From the CD *Change of Direction*
Recorded by Ellen Fullman, Terra Nova Digital Audio
Ⓟ 1996 Ellen Fullman, BMI

15. Uakti

Arrumacao (5:19)
Composed by Elomar Figueria
From the CD *Trilobyte*
Dunvagen Music Publishing
Recorded by Michael Riesman
Ⓟ 1996 Point Music, ASCAP

16. Leonard Solomon

The Grand Gallope (0:56)
Composed by Jacques Offenbach
Ⓟ 1997 Leonard Solomon

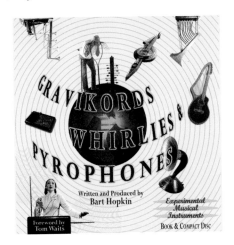

ellipsis arts...

P.O. Box 305, Roslyn, NY 11576
Phone: (800) 788-6670 Fax: (516) 621-2727
Email: Elliarts@aol.com